VOLCANOES

Jennifer Nault

www.av2books.com

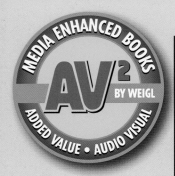

BOOK CODE

N916361

AV² **by Weigl** brings you media enhanced books that support active learning.

AV² provides enriched content that supplements and complements this book. Weigl's AV² books strive to create inspired learning and engage young minds for a total learning experience.

Go to **www.av2books.com**, and enter this book's unique code. You will have access to video, audio, web links, quizzes, a slide show, and activities.

Audio
Listen to sections of the book read aloud.

Video
Watch informative video clips.

Web Link
Find research sites and play interactive games.

Try This!
Complete activities and hands-on experiments.

Due to the dynamic nature of the Internet, some of the URLs and activities provided as part of AV² by Weigl may have changed or ceased to exist. AV² by Weigl accepts no responsibility for any such changes. All media enhanced books are regularly monitored to update addresses and sites in a timely manner. Contact AV² by Weigl at 1-866-649-3445 or av2books@weigl.com with any questions, comments, or feedback.

Published by AV² by Weigl
350 5th Avenue, 59th Floor
New York, NY 10118
Website: www.av2books.com   www.weigl.com

Nault, Jennifer.
 Volcanoes / Jennifer Nault.
     p. cm. -- (Earth science)
 Includes index.
 ISBN 978-1-60596-970-1 (hardcover : alk. paper) -- ISBN 978-1-60596-971-8 (softcover : alk. paper) --
 ISBN 978-1-60596-972-5 (e-book)
 1. Volcanoes--Juvenile literature. 2. Volcanism--Juvenile literature. I. Title.
 QE521.3.N3852 2010
 551.21--dc22
                              2009050236

Printed in the United States of America in North Mankato, Minnesota
1 2 3 4 5 6 7 8 9 0 14 13 12 11 10

052010
WEP042110

Project Coordinator Heather C. Hudak
Design Terry Paulhus

Every reasonable effort has been made to trace ownership and to obtain permission to reprint copyright material. The publishers would be pleased to have any errors or omissions brought to their attention so that they may be corrected in subsequent printings.

Weigl acknowledges Getty Images as its primary image supplier for this title.

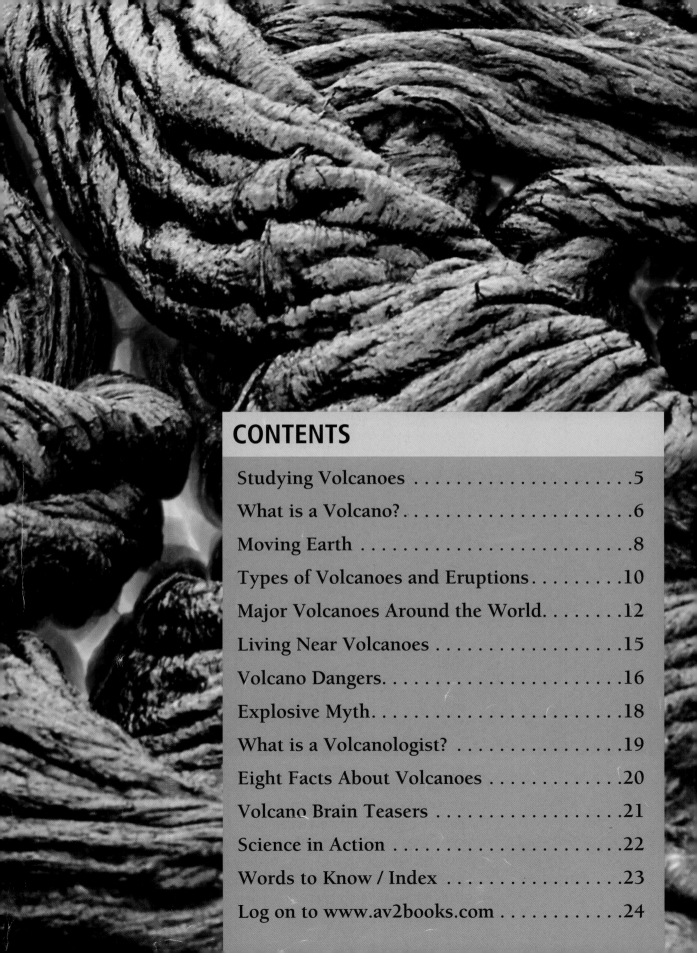

CONTENTS

Eco Notes

In 79 AD, the Italian volcano Vesuvius **erupted**. The ash and dust from the explosion completely covered the Roman town of Pompeii. The people, buildings, and even paintings were perfectly preserved beneath the ash until the buried city was discovered in 1748. This city gives archaeologists a glimpse of daily life in the Roman Empire almost 2,000 years ago. Today, people study volcanoes to try to **predict** when giant eruptions will happen.

Studying Volcanoes

An erupting volcano is an impressive sight to see. When a volcano erupts, gases and dust fly into the sky. Falling ash and red-hot **lava** cover large areas. These materials can destroy everything they touch. An erupting volcano can put people who live nearby in great danger.

Volcanoes erupt because of powerful forces at work deep inside Earth. Scientists are not sure what causes these forces to occur. They study volcanoes to solve this mystery.

The United States is home to several active volcanoes. Earth's largest volcano is Mauna Loa. It rises 2.5 miles (4 kilometers) above sea level. Mauna Loa covers about half of the island of Hawai'i. Kilauea overlaps part of Mauna Loa on the southernmost portion of the island. Kilauea is one of Earth's most active volcanoes. Mount St. Helens in Washington state is also an active volcano. Crater Peak sits atop Mount Spurr in Alaska. It is the **crater** of an active volcano that began erupting at least 6,000 years ago.

■ Materials spurting out of a volcano are very hot. They are about 1,300 to 2,200 degrees Fahrenheit (700 to 1,200 degrees Celsius). This is hot enough to cook a hot dog in one second.

What is a Volcano?

A volcano is an opening in Earth's surface. All volcanoes share some common features.

Earth's interior is extremely hot. It is hot enough to melt rocks and metal, forming **magma**. As rock begins to melt, gas is released. This gas mixes with magma. The gas can make the magma light enough that it rises to Earth's surface. Magma collects in the chamber under a volcano.

As more and more magma enters the chamber, pressure builds. Magma eventually bursts through a passage in Earth's surface called a **vent**. The amount of gas in magma affects eruptions. The more gas there is in magma, the more violent the eruption. Magma that reaches Earth's surface through the crater is called lava. Dried lava forms the volcano's outer layers, or **crust**.

Over time, new vents will appear in the walls of a volcano. As a result of these variations, volcanoes are not all the same. They can look very different depending on what kinds of eruptions they have and when they have them.

PART OF A VOLCANO

1 Vent
Vents are weak parts of the chamber that have been melted or broken by the heat of magma.

2 Secondary Vent
Secondary vents are smaller branches that form in the main vent as magma and gas rise.

3 Crater
A crater is a circular and funnel-shaped opening of a volcano. It is usually found at the top of a cone-shaped mountain.

4 Lava
Once magma reaches Earth's surface, it is called lava. Layers of lava form volcanoes. The size and shape of a volcano depend on the lava's thickness. The thickness of lava depends on how much iron is mixed in with the melted rock.

5 Crust
The crust is dried lava that forms a volcano's outer layers.

6 Magma Chamber
Magma is **molten** rock that rises through the main vent and bursts forth. Magma pools beneath Earth's surface in an area called the magma chamber.

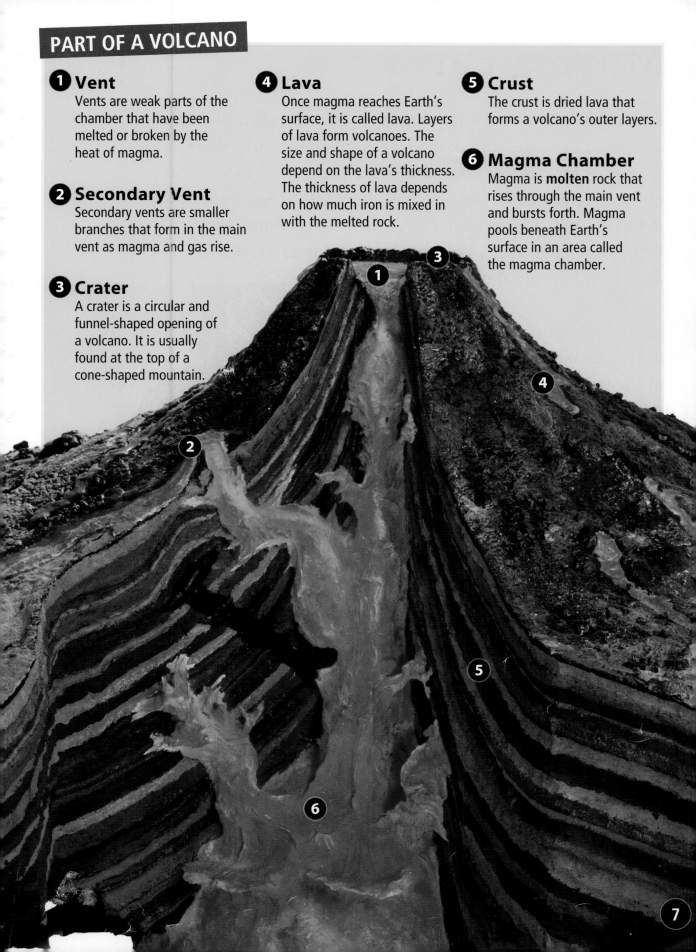

Moving Earth

Earth's surface is made of a thin layer of rock called the crust. The crust is broken into large pieces called tectonic plates. A river of hot magma flows under the plates. The movement of the magma causes the plates to slowly shift. Sometimes, the plates move away from each other. Other times, they hit against each other. Volcanoes can occur as a result of this underground movement.

Even the smallest plates can cause a great deal of damage. For example, movement of the small Juan de Fuca plate is known to cause frequent **tremors** and volcanoes in the area near Washington state.

There are 12 large plates and many smaller plates. Each plate has a different shape and is 4 to 25 miles (6 to 40 km) thick. Most of the plates are made up of both land and ocean crust.

The Pacific Plate is the largest tectonic plate and is almost completely ocean crust. The Nazca and Cocos plates also are mainly made up of ocean crust. The North American, South American, Eurasian, African, Australian, and Antarctic plates are named for the continents they include.

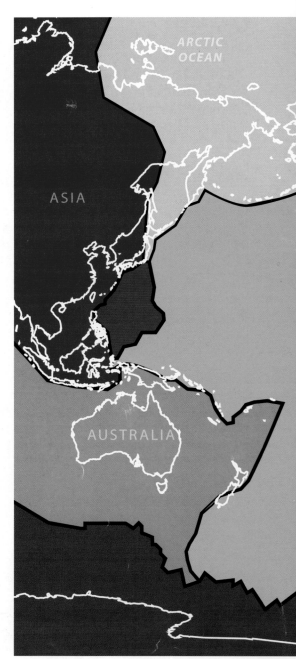

LOCATION OF TECTONIC PLATES

This map shows the location of tectonic plates in relation to Earth's oceans and continents. The colorful patches indicate the shape of the plates. The white outlines the continents in relation to the plates.

LEGEND

- African Plate
- Antarctic Plate
- Arabian Plate
- Australian Plate
- Caribbean Plate
- Cocos Plate
- Eurasian Plate
- Indian Plate
- Juan de Fuca Plate
- Nazca Plate
- North American Plate
- Pacific Plate
- Philippine Plate
- Scotia Plate
- South American Plate

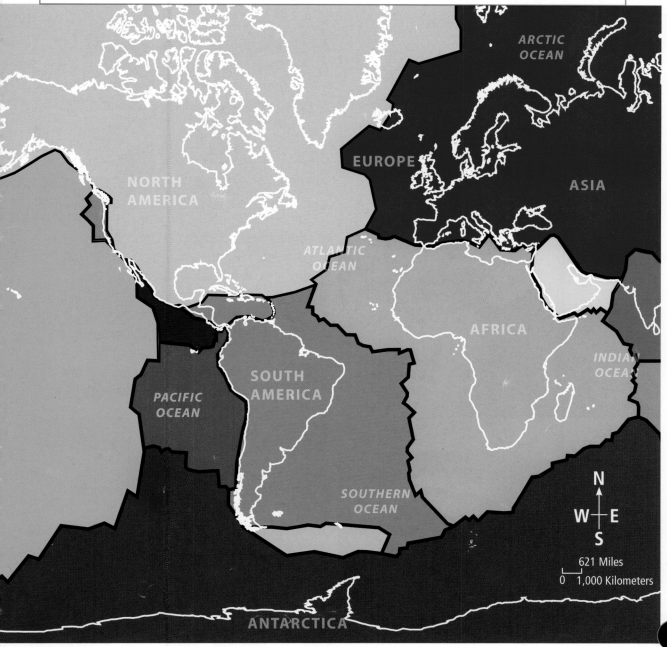

Types of Volcanoes and Eruptions

Scientists group volcanoes into three main types. The types are cinder cones, composite volcanoes, and shield volcanoes.

CINDER CONES

- Cinder cones are steep and cone-like in shape.
- They are formed from tiny, glassy pieces of volcanic rock. These pieces settle around the vent.

COMPOSITE VOLCANOES

- Composite volcanoes are also cone-shaped. They are larger than cinder cones because they have erupted many times from the same vent.
- Composite volcanoes are made from alternating layers of lava, volcanic ash, and cinders. Cinders are pieces of coal, wood, or other material that are still hot and glowing, but no longer burning.

SHIELD VOLCANOES

- Shield volcanoes look like large mounds of earth and rock.
- They are created by runny lava that has a great deal of iron in it and forms **basalt**. Runny lava flows quite far. It creates soft-sloped mountains, such as those found in Hawai'i.

There are different ways that volcanoes can erupt. Some eruptions are very powerful and destructive. Others are weak and cause less damage.

ACTIVE, DORMANT, AND EXTINCT VOLCANOES

- Active volcanoes have erupted in the past few hundred years.
- If a volcano has not erupted for a few hundred years, but has erupted in the last several thousand years, it is called dormant.
- An extinct volcano is a volcano that has not erupted for several thousand years.

EXPLOSIVE ERUPTIONS

- Some eruptions eject liquid, partly solid lava, and pieces of rock. These eruptions are called explosive eruptions.
- Sometimes, these eruptions can last several hours. Other times, they last for days.
- Explosive eruptions have the power of many bombs going off at once.

NONEXPLOSIVE ERUPTIONS

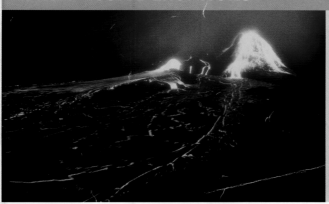

- Nonexplosive eruptions happen when lava is thin so that gases inside it flow freely.
- Streams of lava leak from the top and sides of a volcano. The lava flows downhill and can destroy anything in its path.

Major Volcanoes Around the World

ARCTIC OCEAN

NORTH AMERICA

Katmai

Iliamna

Mount Rainier

Mount St. Helens

PACIFIC OCEAN

Hekla
Helgafell
Surtsey
Eyjafjallajökull

ATLANTIC OCEAN

El Chichón

Paricutin

Mauna Loa
Kilauea

Popocatépetl
Cotopaxi

Cosiguina

Mount Pelée
La Soufrière

SOUTH AMERICA

Villarrica

N
W—E
S

621 Miles
0   1,000 Kilometers

LEGEND

VOLCANOES

WHAT HAVE YOU LEARNED ABOUT VOLCANOES?

This map shows the location of major volcanoes around the world.
Use this map, and research online to answer these questions.
1. Which continent has the most volcanoes?
2. Which continent has the fewest volcanoes?

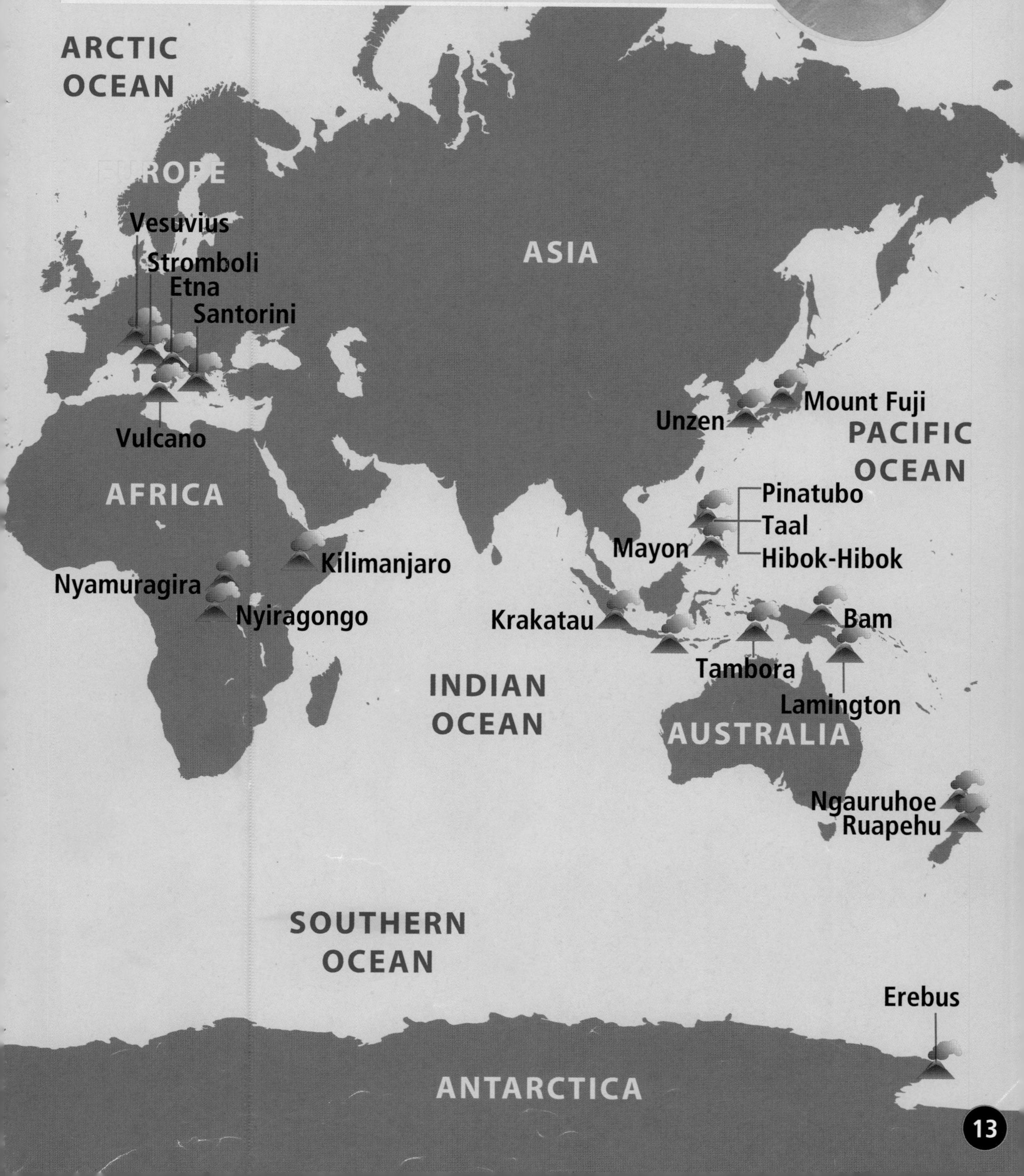

ARCTIC
OCEAN

EUROPE

Vesuvius

Stromboli
Etna
Santorini

Vulcano

AFRICA

Nyamuragira

Nyiragongo

Kilimanjaro

ASIA

Unzen

Mount Fuji

PACIFIC
OCEAN

Pinatubo
Taal
Hibok-Hibok

Mayon

Krakatau

Bam

Tambora

Lamington

INDIAN
OCEAN

AUSTRALIA

Ngauruhoe
Ruapehu

SOUTHERN
OCEAN

Erebus

ANTARCTICA

When Mount St. Helens erupted in 1980, its blast flung rocks at speeds of more than 250 miles (402 km) per hour.

Living Near Volcanoes

Imagine living near a volcano. Most active volcanoes are found around the Pacific Ocean. The volcanoes form a pattern along the edges of the tectonic plates. As a group, these volcanoes are called the "**Ring of Fire**." Mount St. Helens is located in Washington state. This mountain is near the Pacific Coast. It is part of the Cascade Range in the Ring of Fire.

Mount St. Helens erupted on May 18, 1980. A huge explosion spewed gas and ash 12 miles (19 km) into the air. Fifty-seven people died. Many plants and animals were also killed. A large piece of the mountain tore off. Before Mount St. Helens erupted, it was 9,760 feet (2,975 meters) tall. After, it was 8,525 feet (2,598 m) tall.

VOLCANOES IN THE CASCADE RANGE

The Cascade Range spans across the western United States and Canada, from northern California to British Columbia. The range is made up of both volcanic and non-volcanic mountains. Most of the best-known eruptions in the continental United States have happened in the Cascades in the Ring of Fire. This chart shows major eruptions in the Cascades over the past 4,000 years.

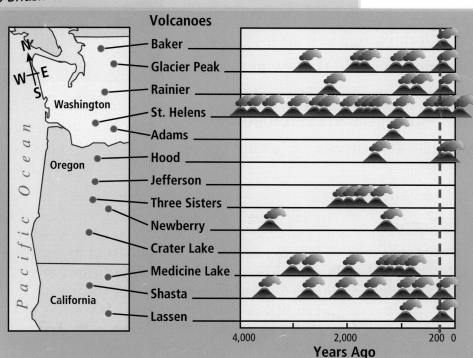

Volcano Dangers

People who live near active volcanoes face many frightening hazards. Ash and dust can cover large areas. They can destroy crops and plant life. They can also kill people. Some types of lava flow very quickly. People do not always have time to leave the area. Hot lava can cause harm to living things.

Gases are released into the **atmosphere** during an eruption. These gases can be poisonous. People may die if they breathe in the gas.

Mudflows caused by an eruption are known as lahars. They are caused when rain mixes with ash. Lahars destroy everything in their path. Underwater volcanoes cause tidal waves. These waves are called tsunamis. Tsunamis can flood coastal areas. Flooding damages structures and harms people.

In 2009, an undersea volcano off the coast of Tonga erupted, sending ash and smoke up to 328 feet (100 m) in the air.

One of the largest volcanic eruptions in history is believed to have happened around 1500 BC on the Greek island of Santorini. Even 19 miles (31 km) away from the blast, piles of ash and debris were up to 100 feet (30 m) high. The explosion was so large that it likely destroyed most of the island that originally held the volcano. It is thought that this explosion might have been the beginning of the stories of Atlantis, a mythical city that sunk beneath the ocean.

Volcanic Eruptions Through Time

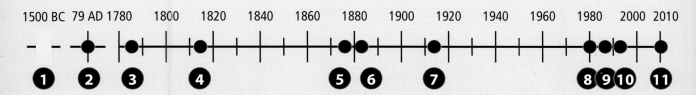

1500 BC 79 AD 1780 1800 1820 1840 1860 1880 1900 1920 1940 1960 1980 2000 2010

1 **2** **3** **4** **5** **6** **7** **8** **9** **10** **11**

1 Around 1500 BC
A major volcano eruption happens in Santorini, Greece. The eruption becomes the subject of many myths.

2 79 AD
Mount Vesuvius erupts, burying the cities of Pompeii and Stabiae.

1783
Laki, a volcanic vent in Iceland, erupts about 10 times in 8 months.

4 1815
Mount Tambora in Indonesia erupts in a massive explosion. It is the largest known eruption in history. The eruption triggers a tsunami.

5 1877
Cotopaxi, a volcano in the Ring of Fire, erupts and causes a major landslide.

6 1882
Galunggung Volcano in Indonesia erupts, causing 4,011 deaths.

7 1914–1921
Lassen Peak in California erupts several times over the span of three years. The most harmful eruption happens on May 19, 1915. The ash cloud rises 7 miles (11 km) into the air.

8 1980
Mount St. Helens in Washington erupts on May 18. The destructive eruption is triggered by an earthquake underneath the volcano.

9 1984
Mauna Loa erupts on March 25. The eruption lasts for three weeks.

10 1991
The eruption of Mount Pinatubo in the Philippines kills 300 people. It is the largest eruption of the 20th century.

11 2010
Eyjafjallajökull erupts in Iceland. Ash from the volcano shuts down airlines across Europe, affecting millions of travelers around the world.

Explosive Myth

Volcanoes are named after Vulcan, the Roman god of fire. Early Romans believed that Vulcan lived beneath Vulcano Island, which is just north of Sicily.

Early Romans found a smoking island off the coast of Sicily. They believed the god of fire made lightning deep inside the island. They named the island Vulcano. The island is still there today.

■ The last time the small volcanic island of Vulcano erupted was in 1890. More than 470 people now live there.

What is a Volcanologist?

A volcanologist is a special type of **geologist**. Volcanologists can predict volcanic eruptions. What they learn can save lives. Volcanologists track volcanic activity using **observatories** and maps. They study volcanic rock in laboratories.

An important tool used to study volcanoes is a seismometer. This tool measures tremors in the ground and helps scientists predict eruptions. Volcanologists use **lasers** to record changes in the ground around volcanoes and video cameras to capture eruptions.

Haroun Tazieff

Tazieff was a well-known French volcanologist. He often put himself in danger to learn more about volcanoes. He wrote books and made films on the subject. One of his documentaries was nominated for an **Oscar**.

WORKING CONDITIONS

A volcanologist's work can be dangerous. Sometimes, volcanologists study active volcanoes.

SAFETY

Volcanologists wear thermal suits while studying active volcanoes. These suits help keep out heat. Temperatures can reach 1,868 degrees Fahrenheit (1,020°C) at the Ertale Volcano in Ethiopia.

Eight Facts About Volcanoes

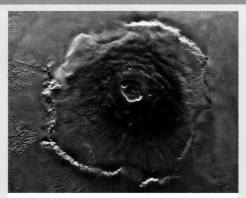

Mars has the largest volcano in the solar system. Olympus Mons is three times the height of Mount Everest.

There are two kinds of lava. Fluid lava, called pahoehoe, flows quickly. Sticky lava, called a'a, moves more slowly.

In the past 10,000 years, 1,500 volcanoes have erupted.

Volcanoes helped create Earth. They added new rock to the land and gases to the atmosphere.

Some of the best-known igneous rocks are basalt, granite, pumice, and obsidian.

There are more than 1,500 active volcanoes in the world today.

Jupiter's moon Io is the most volcanic place in the solar system.

Volcanoes are most often located along continental borders, island chains, and in undersea ranges.

Volcano Brain Teasers

1 What is the name of the group of volcanoes found along the Pacific Ocean?

2 What is magma called when it is outside of a volcano?

3 What is the name of Earth's largest volcano?

4 What kind of volcano is formed by an eruption of basalt lava?

5 What is a scientist who studies volcanoes called?

6 What is the name for volcanic rock?

7 There are two types of volcano hazards. True or false?

8 When did a huge eruption take place on Mount St. Helens?

9 What is the name for mudflows caused by an eruption?

10 What tool is used to measure volcanic tremors?

ANSWERS: 1. Ring of Fire 2. Lava 3. Mauna Loa 4. Shield volcano 5. A volcanologist 6. Igneous rock 7. False. There are more than five types of volcano hazards. 8. May 18, 1980 9. Lahars 10. A seismometer

Science in Action

Make Your Own Volcano

This activity should be done with an adult.

Tools Needed

foam tray

newspapers

scissors

cone-shaped party hat

empty film canister

papier-mâché

1 tablespoon (15 ml) of baking soda

toothpick

red vinegar

Directions

1 Place the foam tray on a table covered with newspapers. Cut a hole in the top of the party hat. Fit the film canister snugly into the hole. Set the hat on the tray. Be sure the opening of the film canister faces the ceiling.

2 Cover the hat and tray with papier-mâché. Do not cover the opening of the film canister. Let the volcano dry overnight.

3 Put the baking soda into the top of the volcano. Poke a few holes in the baking soda with a toothpick. Pour red vinegar into the top of the volcano.

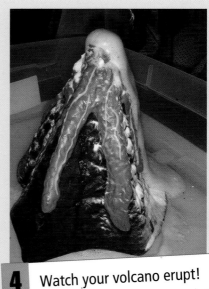

4 Watch your volcano erupt!

Words to Know

atmosphere: air; a mixture of gases surrounding Earth

basalt: a type of volcanic rock that is hard, black, and often glassy

crater: a circular and funnel-shaped opening of a volcano

crust: dried lava that forms a volcano's outer layers

erupted: ejected gas, steam, ash, or lava with great force

geologist: a person who studies the material and structure of Earth

lasers: devices that make very thin and strong beams of light

lava: hot, melted rock that comes out of an erupting volcano

magma: very hot liquid rock deep inside Earth

molten: an object that heat has turned into a liquid form

observatories: places that have telescopes used for studying the Sun, the Moon, planets, stars, or volcanoes

Oscar: an award for achievement in a motion picture

predict: to say that something will happen based on what is already known about how similar events work

Ring of Fire: an area around the Pacific Ocean where volcanoes form a pattern along the edges of the tectonic plates

tremors: shakes

vent: an opening from which gases or volcanic material escapes

Index

Log on to www.av2books.com

AV² by Weigl brings you media enhanced books that support active learning. Go to **www.av2books.com**, and enter the special code inside the front cover of this book. You will gain access to enriched and enhanced content that supplements and complements this book. Content includes video, audio, web links, quizzes, a slide show, and activities.

Audio
Listen to sections of the book read aloud.

Video
Watch informative video clips.

Web Link
Find research sites and play interactive games.

Try This!
Complete activities and hands-on experiments.

WHAT'S ONLINE?

Try This! Complete activities and hands-on experiments.	**Web Link** Find research sites and play interactive games.	**Video** Watch informative video clips.	**EXTRA FEATURES**
Pages 6-7 Test your knowledge of the parts of a volcano.	**Pages 4-5** Find out where volcanoes are found around the world.	**Pages 4-5** Take a tour of volcanoes around the world.	**Audio** Hear introductory audio at the top of every page
Pages 8-9 Test your knowledge of places where tectonic plates are found around the world.	**Pages 10-11** Learn more about volcanoes.	**Pages 10-11** Learn about different types of volcanoes and how they form.	
Pages 12-13 Complete a mapping activity about the major volcanoes of the world.	**Pages 12-13** Discover the top 10 volcanoes in history.	**Pages 16-17** Learn about the dangers people face living near volcanoes.	**Key Words** Study vocabulary, and play a matching word game.
Page 14-15 Test your knowledge of volcanoes that have erupted in the past 4,000 years.	**Pages 14-15** Learn about volcanic hazards.	**Pages 18-19** Watch a researcher describing her first experience working on a volcano.	
Pages 16-17 Describe the dangers of a volcano.	**Pages 20-21** Find out how you can become a volcanologist.		**Slide Show** View images and captions, and try a writing activity.
Pages 18-19 Write a description about how researchers can predict a volcano's future.			
Pages 20-21 Test your volcano knowledge.			
Page 22 Build your own volcano, and play an interactive game.			

Due to the dynamic nature of the Internet, some of the URLs and activities provided as part of AV² by Weigl may have changed or ceased to exist. AV² by Weigl accepts no responsibility for any such changes. All media enhanced books are regularly monitored to update addresses and sites in a timely manner. Contact AV² by Weigl at 1-866-649-3445 or av2books@weigl.com with any questions, comments, or feedback.

Welcome to AV² by Weigl!